Flowers the

in the Snow

By Holly Kerr

Illustrated by Kirsten Smith

In memory of my mum,
Debbie Wiltshire Kerr.

I will hold you in my heart
for the rest of my days,
because death may have
ended your life,
but it can never
end my love.

Contents

Broken Petals

Watching someone you love slowly die
from cancer is like being unable to stop
the sand slipping through an hourglass;
every day, another piece of them
falls away until there's
nothing left—
long before
they take
their last
breath.

You turned being broken into art,
mending your cracks with gold
until you became
stronger
than ever before.

Kintsugi

Every day after
your diagnosis
when I would hold
you in my arms,
I only ever had
one thought
running through
my mind:

*Please don't
let the ground
hold you like this.*

When the sun starts to
bleed into the night
and we fear your
chest may not
rise with the dawn,
you tell me:
"Even when there is
nothing but darkness,
you, my little light seeker,
are always surrounded
by stars, if only you look up."

Even though you will
never know my daughter,
she will grow up knowing you.
She will learn to never
fear the shadows just
like you taught me to.

Little light seekers

The light is fading
from your eyes
and I can do nothing
but watch your life
being cut short
like a winter sunset.

I grew up believing
you were a magician
when you would make
everything I ever needed
appear out of thin air.
I just never imagined
the show would
end like this,
that your final trick
would be a
vanishing act.

You were given just a
10% survival rate,
and while that
eclipsed all my hope,
you told me that
only some flowers are
strong enough to plant
roots in the ice.
Not all will survive—
but those that do will
forever wear the sun
as a crown.

Now, every time
I see a snowdrop
I want to scream
why couldn't that
have been you?

One day, you will endure
a pain so strong that
it will feel like your entire
universe has been rearranged,
while the rest of the world
somehow continues to
turn— unchanged.

Life after loss

Losing you pulled
at my heartstrings
until I entirely unravelled,
and now I don't know
how to stitch myself
back together again.

I often wonder why I feel
so empty all the time,
but then I remember
that my heart
no longer rests
inside my chest:
it followed you
six feet under.

Dead girl walking

How many more
shooting stars
must I wish on
to bring you
back to me?

Take me back to
the last time I got to
tell you that I loved you.
I would hold your hand
just that little bit tighter.
I would never let you go.

The movie's over,
the end credits have
finished rolling,
but I can't stop wishing
I could rewind to the
opening scene and
watch it all again
just one more time.

Every night,
I talk to the moon.
Every night,
I tell her about you.
If only you could
hear me too.

The history of you
fits inside a small box:
faded photos full of smiles,
your wedding ring,
postcards from every
city you visited,
concert stubs
and your favourite CD's,
the shells we collected from
trips to the beach,
that one book you read
so many times
that the pages started
falling out.

How can a human soul weigh so little?

I clutch the photographs
I still have of us
close to my chest.
It's the only way
I'm able to hold you
after you left.

Like a night without the stars,
a morning without the sunrise,
a flower without its petals—
I am incomplete without you.

I'm lost,
because the place
I once called home
no longer exists.

Homesick for a heart that's stopped beating

Like a lipstick stain
on my white shirt,
losing you left a mark
on my heart that can
never be washed away.

Some scars are sealed with a kiss

Grief was the thief
of all I held dear,
for I didn't just lose you,
I lost myself too.

After you left, I packed my bags
and moved into a new flat,
in a new city,
and I got a new job,
but I can't help feeling guilty
because I get to carry on living
and making new memories
while your eyes are forever shut.

But then I picture you smiling and
I can hear you saying:
"You don't have to stop loving me,
but you must let me go.
How can you welcome
tomorrow with open arms
if you are still busy
holding hands with yesterday?
How can you carry on living for us both?"

I need to turn the page
and start the next chapter,
but it's so hard
to carry on reading
when the plot has
lost all meaning.

At least
in my dreams,
we get to meet
once more.

Even after all
this time apart,
I still feel your
presence
everywhere
I go.

It's not
the forever
I planned
for us.

I remember learning
in chemistry class
that energy
cannot be destroyed;
it simply changes form.
That's how I know
your spirit is never lost.
It lives on in the
hearts of those who
loved you.

May your heart
continue to beat
in every word
of poetry
I write.

Can you ever truly die if
you are loved by a writer?

You spent a lifetime
planting seeds of love
in my heart
until my soul was
filled with the
most vibrant garden.
It's only now
I realise you were
preparing me
for this day
when you could
no longer be
with me to
nurture my petals.

I must be strong enough to bloom
for us both

Seeking Sunlight

The world was so scared
you would fly too high
that you became scared of it too.
You let them bring you
back down to the ground
where you never belonged.

Dear reader, what happened to your wings?

Healing isn't always pretty.
At first it looks a lot like
sleepless nights,
eyes too dry
to cry another tear,
declined phone calls,
cancelled plans,
feeling stuck beneath
the crushing weight
of living.

It's okay to take your
time in this phase,
for not even the moon
can complete
its cycle overnight.

Healing isn't always pretty,
but the end view will be.

Be kind to yourself:
like a wildflower in spring,
each day you are growing
just that little bit more.

Uproot all the
seeds of doubt
from your mind
and plant only
thoughts of
adoration,
for there is
such strength
in simply
surviving.

Sometimes
you need
a storm
to wash
away all the
debris so
you can see
clearly again.

Grief is still an
unwelcome guest
that stops by to
visit me when
I least expect it,
but it's no longer a
permanent resident
in my heart.

Evicting grief

You may feel
broken now,
but one day
not even the
strongest chains
will be able to
hold you back.

They will tell you
it's impossible,
but be resilient
and continue to
grow where
people least
expect you to—
even if that means
growing alone.
Just look at how
much stronger
you are
for it now.

Flowers that bloom in the snow

Don't ever hide
your scars.
They tell a
story of the
survivor you are.

I'll take these tears
and sprinkle them
over the daffodils,
so new beginnings
can sprout from the
ruins of my despair.

On your darkest days,
look to the stars:
they too burn out
before they can
shine their brightest.

The world may have taken
everything from me,
but I will never let it
take my kindness.

Weave these dandelions
into a crown of flowers,
and remind them that
you can be both
beautiful and strong.

Rewriting fairytales

Dear 2021,
thank you for
teaching me that
life often feels
unconquerable,
but just maybe,
so am I.

The seasons never
apologise for changing
and neither should you.
Only by changing can
you grow anew.

It takes billions
of years for a
diamond to form
from carbon,
so be patient
with yourself
as you learn
to reach your
full potential.

You were born
to become the
protagonist
in your story,
not the
side character.

You've spent
far too long
being afraid to
take up space
when you deserve
to stand so tall.

I was told I
could grow up
to be anything
I wanted to be,
so I've decided
I'll become
enough for myself
before anybody else.

Don't feel pressured
to grow where your
roots anchor you:
have the courage to
seek out your own soil
and bloom where you
choose to plant yourself.

I won't ever tame the
tide inside my heart
just because others can't swim.
I am a child of nature and
my power must be set free.

I'm like the moon:
all of my phases
are worthy.

.

The art you create
does not solely
determine your value.
You yourself are
a masterpiece
to be revered.

Never take a poet for granted:
their pen has the power
to sow seeds of joy
or uproot an entire woodland.

What a shame it is
that you wasted so
much time looking
elsewhere when you
already had everything
you needed within
your heart to flourish;
these seeds just needed to
be watered and nourished.

The entire world
is at your fingertips—
as long as you have the
courage to reach for
what is rightfully yours.

You look
so radiant
now you've
started wearing
hope like your
favourite dress.
Don't ever take it off.

Never again doubt
your worth:
like the sun,
you brighten
every life
you touch
without even
realising it.

Each version
of yourself
is a fossil
in the museum
of your past
that deserves to be
displayed with pride.

Stop draining yourself
every day by looking in the
mirror and seeing only the pieces
of yourself you feel you have
to hide to please the world;
all the time spent agonising
over not being
slim enough,
tall enough,
curvy enough,
good enough.

It's time to smash
the mirror and let
your true self seep
out from between
the cracks.

Set yourself free

Cease trying to fit in
when wildflowers were
born to teach us
that there is such
beauty in *diversity*.

Forget about seeking perfection:
embrace each and every one
of your flaws,
for they make you
perfectly human.

Your value
rests not
upon your
skin,
but comes
from deep
within.

The greatest love story
ever written
is the tale of a
young girl finally
feeling brave enough
to fall in love
with the person
she is becoming.

My dear body,
let me apologise to you
for all the times I forgot
I didn't need to be
anybody else
to be beautiful;
I was beautiful all along.

Now, when I picture
the girl I want to become,
she's already smiling
back at me in the mirror
saying, "*welcome home.*"

Is this what finding yourself feels like?

Sharing Soil

For too long,
I built the walls
around myself so high
until I was
untouchable
in my
castle in the sky.
But hearts grow
cold in solitude,
and over time
what was left of mine
turned to stone.

Eventually, the drawbridge
must be lowered to let love back in

Love is the world's
most valuable currency,
so invest only in those
who will spend it wisely.
Don't ever let others
leave you bankrupt
while they relish
in your riches.

You came into my life
like the first day of summer,
and I smiled because I
knew my heart would
finally remember
what it felt like
to be warm.

We clicked
like Lego bricks,
and assembled all
of our broken pieces
into an unshakeable tower.

Let's see how high this love can take us

Forever was a
long-lost dream
until I met you.
Now, in your eyes,
I see the promise
of tomorrow
I've always been
searching for.

& suddenly,
all the sonnets
I have only ever
read and dreamt
about,
make sense.

Our love story
will never end,
hearts lingering
together,
upon every page
forever.

You say I'm wild,
and for the first time
it no longer sounds
like a bad thing.

Sew me into every
fibre of your heart.
Let your blood
become
my life source.
Let each beat
strengthen me.

Fall into my arms
like the sunset
into the horizon,
and let the rising
stars guide
your fingers
to my heart.

Let me get lost in
your golden soul,
until I no longer
need to watch
the sunrise
to feel the light
finally
returning to my heart.

I knew I was in love
the night we camped
beneath the stars.
Your eyes had been fixed
solely on the view,
while I couldn't help
looking only at you.

Don't settle in love
when it's meant to
make your soul soar.

Find someone
who makes
falling feel
like flying.

Every time I worry that
I'm not enough,
you tell me I'm like
the air you breathe,
that I'm everything
you'll ever need.

You deserve to be
loved by someone
who wants you
to be nothing
but yourself.

Kiss me like
we have all the
time in the world.
Let's make our
own little infinity
together.

Grow between my bones—
fill in my cracks with petals,
so we can bloom together
into a beautiful Eden,
forever facing the sun.

One day, you'll
meet someone
who undresses
your heart before
their fingers ever
touch your body,
and you'll discover
what true intimacy
feels like.

I don't need a
grand adventure
to be happy,
just you and I together
on a quiet
Sunday afternoon,
where my entire world
fits inside our
cosy living room.

Your eager kisses
join my scars into the
most beautiful constellation,
and I shine brighter than
I ever knew I could.

I know your body
like a worn map.
By candlelight,
I explore worlds
I've already voyaged to
and set foot upon new horizons.
I can get lost in you,
but I know I'm never truly lost,
for each path always leads me
straight back to your heart.

Your touch is like
a honeyed hymn,
and I can't help
but sing softly
to every sweet note.

Between dusk and dawn,
satin sheets are our stage,
and you are
my puppet-master,
pulling my strings
just right
until I become
your most
beautiful show.

Your body fits
against mine
like poetry's
most perfect rhyme.

Together, we are breathing art

You are a dream
I never have to
wake up from.

Tomorrow isn't promised,
so I won't wait until
Valentine's day
to tell you that I love you:
I'll remind you every night
before you fall asleep,
and I'll hold you
close every morning I
am lucky enough to
share with you.

You are
the light
in a world
full of
darkness.

One lifetime with you
simply isn't long enough.
May our hearts meet
in every world hereafter.

It's beautiful
when two hearts
fit together
so perfectly,
like the missing
pieces of a puzzle
finally falling
into place—
finally complete.

About the author

In 2021, Holly graduated from the University of Edinburgh with a first class master's degree in English and Scottish Literature. After graduating, she started writing poetry which has since been featured in various anthologies and magazines. To read more of her work, find her on Instagram: @hollykerr.poetry.

Printed in Great Britain
by Amazon

80669327R00068